Melisma

Lana Al Habl

BookLeaf
Publishing

Presentation by *BookLeaf Publishing*

Web: www.bookleafpub.com

E-mail: info@bookleafpub.com

ISBN: 9789357692182

First edition 2022

*To my father, who always said he'd publish
my words.*

Calendar

Observe this tree from my balcony; it exists in its own time, as well as mine.

Days will turn, hours will accumulate, weeks will recycle themselves, and it will endure; on the periphery of my awareness.

Then one day I will notice it.

Immediately, it is lush and flowering, verdant signaling spring. Life... time.

Then I'll notice it again.

Instantly its amber leaves clutch at the arms that carry it.

Hours...weeks... I'll notice it again.

Struck by its bold bareness, branches stripped clean, turned skeletal while I exist only metres away from it.

I'm being reminded
over and over

of the cyclical character of our existence
as if what is present can only be so to perish,
into a memory eternal.

Blue

I am blue. Cerulean. Indigo. The transparent, tepid blue at the bottom of a bath. The dazzling white-blue capped mountains. The navy of... a lost soul.

Photograph

Tonight's evening is still. Stoic palm trees have seemingly frozen in space, white noise has replaced the wind and the usually frenetic bats are peering silently from their perch.

How eerie to be found in this snapshot.

For the first time, I'm the only one in flux. Even the clouds are asleep. What are they waiting for? What am I waiting for?

The more I move, the more untroubled my surrounding scenes seem. Barely a leaf trembles. It's a trick, I'm sure of it. An optical illusion.

I should go inside and cause a ruckus.

Rose

Your silent reach I see, as you search your inside
pockets, and I will run from your approach,
infinite strides to my prey-like scarper.

I will dodge as your fingers fumble; the blind
hunting the blind. I want to look back, but your
trophy faces forward in the direction of your
breaths, an anchor point at my ear.

Wrist-deep for what you frisk, your pulse at your
heartbeat, a syncopated search.

I will grasp for what it is you search for, face
forwards my trophy. Bring your beats to my
discovery, your bone-white three-piece makes
you an easy target. Follow my breaths toward
what it is you search for; the hunt is up.

There, can you see? That rose as your lapel, the
scarlet that fills your inside pocket where your
fingers once drowned and where I once hid.

Machine

I've lost my poetry, says the cog-like machine. All that is intimate has been stripped bare, flesh flayed for sullen embers to remain. Can you hear murmurings? Familiar nudges, just beyond your outstretched hand.

Will

Tell me what to do and where to do it, but on my own terms.

I ask of you to guide my hand, propel me but hold me loosely.

Pour the paint, but leave it up to the artist, then tell me I did it right.

Speak my thoughts in my own voice. I will wait for you.

Open

As one who has always wrapped herself up in the cocoon consolation of enclosed areas; an emblem of encroaching space and the safety of permanence; walls I can touch; these boarding houses of brick; a soul in a bunker looking up as the assaults of the daily world whizz past our heads…. I have recently found myself drawn to the solace of open spaces instead, both inner and outer.

There is an infiniteness and lightness of being that only a sparse, desolate stretch of space can offer, where one goes to reach the ends of the earth, an end to only begin again.

Great wide plains, fields of canola, arctic icescapes; these are the engorged spaces I now crave.

Pool

If you peer closely enough, and obeserve from
the inside out, if the images are lucent and
motion you to dive in, if the rays of the sun are
tricking you behind closed eyes:

it might just be real.

Keep them shut and lay back on those
sun-drenched tiles, sacrifice an arm for another,
and exchange the fantasy for the inevitibility...

I wait

Not everything is created to be seen.

I learned this perched on the peak above the lake, an amber outline to every shadow, as she rose to expand and reveal, all that cannot be seen.

Who created time? Certainly not this ghost of the mountain, who meanders behind the veil, curious eyes, kind eyes, a noble gaze beyond space and time.

I wait.

I wait for you. I wait as long as I know I wait on your time, as long as my patience is in vain for your revelations, for as long as my linger stretches beyond my desires. There is nothing for me back there. A world stripped clean of mystery and your gaze.

Unmade

His dystopian confessionals have always been of
the times and beyond the times; he flings those
inscrutable electros back and forth all over
again.

Listen, and rid yourself of rationale as the
serpent sheds its veneer, all disrobed and still in
waiting for the scales to envelop its nakedness
once again.

Sail to the moon; a new robe awaits;
one that is unmade,
fling yourself into the electros,
nothing will protect you, as you do not need
protection from yourself.

Restless

There is a fate indeed far paltry than that of
boredom, more sinister than an anxious bout, a
grander detriment than sorrow; that is to suffer
and kneel at the feet of restlessness.

I want to do nothing, but do it all...

Behold that wily, restless imp that tricks and
bends the will, saying to you that a life overhaul
is the only way out.
But gives no tools.
No direction.
Not an ounce of a realstic outlook.

Stone

Woe to her who cannot plant her stake deep into the ground.

The perpetual here nor there is a self-replenishing well, drowning until you are not. Parched, until you are not.

I want to be like a stone that sinks to the bottom of the ultimate well, nestling into the grit and sand until its shape fills the space. Many iterations of water will pass over me, attempting to dislodge, but failing to unearth this fallen treasure.

I want to inhabit this groove my heaviness creates, wearing my barnacles and lichen as badges of perpetuity. Centuries will come and go, civilizations will create and break, yet I will remain unmoved, moored, unchanged but not the same.

Machine

How does something that should, in its own
right, be cold, clinical, and machine-like, how
does it cut through and chat my emotional
landscape like the deft healer it is?

The machines are born of us, these tense,
synthetic lines fashion into forlorn soundscapes
with moments of chaos and tumult; but there is
life to be found in them yet. There is some way
to stumble across our humanness and warmth
along all the codes of lines that dash between us:
so that man and machine can live symbiotically.

The chameleon

The song of the chameleon:

Bend and adapt your ways. Yes, today I'll be a sullen, bookish type partial to long, contemplative pauses for you, and tomorrow I'll be the coquettish charmer for the other. Then there's family me. Work me. Friendship groups me. Customer me. Citizen me. Student me. Me for him. Me for her. Me for them.

I peered into the surface of every lake, yet none of them reflected me.

Weather

A weather forecast:

Pulsing hum of rain, with a chance of melancholia from the space left by the loss of time.

A cheer-defying cold front threatens to topple the recent warmth of country-tinged guitars, while the whispering winds pick up, carrying murmurings of optimism; but you must lean in close to hear them.

Awaken

The vulnerability of the just-awoken:

Before the day itself has smothered you with
distractions, obligations, and shiny, pretty things
to paw at.

Dread leaks into your sleep, and settles heavily
on your consciousness, like a thousand spider
webs, a sticky and tangled trap.

You wake, clawing through the dread web,
assaulted by everything that is wrong, could go
wrong, has gone wrong.

Reach far and close by for excuses to keep you
from the day, from rousing yourself to reality.

And not just of a sunrise, webs that entrap,
awakening from daytime naps offer the same
forbidding fogs.

There is something
about that initial awareness, the awakening, that
unwelcoming realisation that you made it
through the night

unconsciously, and now it's time to make it
through the day with all of your senses blazing.

A friend

She visits daily, perched on the teal metal branch, often facing outward, but momentarily facing inwards; into my house, into her song, above my full awareness but so close to our conjunction.

I have tried many times to capture her, a willing image that cannot translate her song, her peace, and her ecological rhythm of being.

Chaos

Perhaps symmetry in nature exists not only as an axis in and of itself but to halfway satiate our "passion for comprehension" through some visual aid of order; a neat and tidy enlightenment.

Observe, here, this consoling reflection of accuracy, and comprehend the abstract: don't give me all the answers, I will uproot disorder from our clarity of being, I only understand uncertainty as an essential for faring in this predict-less existence.

Remember

I can't recall what he said to me, only the voice in which he said it.

Perhaps it was harsh words, avuncular in length and intent, cutting-deep in delivery. I deserved it, he didn't.

There were always words between us, like tethered script, unspoken but carrying the full load of our relationship. This is what he wanted for me...

My memories are sparse; roving and rotating in my mental album on loop. Spectral father, unmoored recollections, and loose ends.

The secret conformity

22

Take heed, you are in good company. Your heart feels just that little bit further, breaks just that little bit harder, and searches endlessly.